LOST IN TANGLES

LOST IN TANGLES

ACCEPTING NATURAL HAIR

L. B. HAMILTON

HAMWELL BOOKS
Ventura

Copyright © 2018 by L. B. Hamilton
All rights reserved. This book or any portion thereof
may not be reproduced or used in any manner whatsoever
without the express written permission of the publisher
except for the use of brief quotations in a book review.

Printed in the United States of America

First Printing, 2018

ISBN 978-0-692-16986-5

ISBN 978-0-692-16342-9

Hamwell Books
3 Carrillo Street
Santa Barbara, CA 93101

www.lbhamiltonbooks.com

Contents

vii

Introduction   1

Part I. Main Body

1. A Brief History of African American Hair   7
2. The Purpose of Hair   12
3. Self-Worth Wrapped in Self-Image   20
4. Impressionable Youth   26

Part II. PART TWO

5.	My Hair Journey	33
6.	Processed Good or Bad	46
7.	Falling In Love With My Hair	56
8.	Role Model to My Children	63
9.	Other People's Opinion	74
10.	What's Best For You	84
	About The Author	91

For my children,
my mom,
and all young girls struggling to fit
in.

Introduction

In this culture, many African Americans are starting to discover their natural curly hair after years of applying relaxers, hot combs, and flat irons. Many have not seen their natural hair structure since they were little. Generations have perpetuated the cycle of suppressing natural curly hair to fit in, to satisfy the status quo. This new wave hasn't only hit America, it has hit worldwide, extending beyond the community of African descent into

Introduction

other ethnic groups of people with curly or afro hair. There are a great many people outside of the great African diaspora who have persisted on straightening their curly tresses, often on a daily basis, to fit into the set standard this generation has succumbed to however, they are now choosing to embrace their natural hair. It is a good thing that people all over the world are decidedly choosing themselves over the present-day status quo.

Some may be opposed and portray the movement as a temporary phase or trend however, major companies are taking notice on this rapidly growing movement and have stocked store shelves with plenty of curl creams, gels, curl activators and moisturizers for curly hair. The natural hair community

Introduction

began demanding for there to be products created without the harsh chemicals of parabens and silicones, to which the companies quickly responded by creating affordable, paraben and silicone-free hair products, specifically for curly hair.

There is an overabundance of natural hair tutorials on YouTube and other social media outlets which are dedicated to the care and management of natural curly hair alone. There are supporters as well as dissenters who constructively make their opinions known to the world, thereby creating an honest, intriguing dialogue between each other. This has all ripened our hearts to openness and thus, has created such an exciting time in which many of us are discovering another part of ourselves. Fortunately, this openness

INTRODUCTION

has led to people discovering their true selves and it has also enabled them to reflect upon the side of the argument they have chosen to support and stand firm on. This is a guide to encourage you to support and stand firm on your own truth, to understand that what is good for one person isn't necessarily good for another and finally, to encourage anyone to choose whatever may bring them peace and tranquility within, regardless of the opinions of others that may surround you, provided the choice is healthy. We ought to drown out the voices around us to discover the true and quite possibly, hidden wants and desires of our own hearts outside of public opinion and decide to be quite well with it.

Part I

Main Body

I

A BRIEF HISTORY OF AFRICAN AMERICAN HAIR

Styling African hair proved to be of most difficulty during the years of our enslavement. We didn't have access to the hair styling tools, accessories, and products we were accustomed to in Africa that produced elaborate braiding, twisting, and locking hairstyles. Furthermore, I can't foresee anyone taking such a interest in haircare when families all around them, including their own, are being torn apart before their eyes. However, natural oils, butters and herbal treatments were used in Africa whereas in America, many had to resort to leftover cooking oils to nourish their hair. It was to the slave owner to determine the styling of their slaves' hair to which there were various products on the market geared towards straightening African curls.

Africans with naturally straighter hair and lighter skin were priced at a higher rate on the auction block which deemed them better than those with kinkier hair and darker skin. This system has been and continues to be a great division amongst the African diaspora. The internalization of such a system is highly destructive to the self-esteem and self-worth of all ages to which many searched out the straightening products of their slave owners.

This system of supremacy is again perpetuated when schools and businesses require Africans to censor their African characteristics, essentially implementing a forced assimilation not only physically, but in the psychology as well. This forced way of thinking produced the invention of the "hot comb" which straightens the hair. It also produced the first self-made millionaire, Madam C. J. Walker. In the early 1900's, Walker produced hair care products aimed at the maintenance of straightened, African hair however, her line didn't come without much controversy. Many believed Walker to be promoting self-hate in the African community.

Proceeding Walker's line of hair products were the chemical hair straighteners for men and women. And with the rise of black power in the 1970's, along with the afros and dreadlocks, came the chemical hair curler, Jheri Curl.

In the 1980's, braids were once again popular with the invention of artificial hair. With the rise in demand for artificial hair came a demand for wigs, hair tracks and artificial ponytails to which created an empire for Korean artificial hair retailers.

Lost In Tangles

Since the new millenia, African Americans and the African diaspora have looked to themselves to determine the way in which they are to wear their hair, be it straightened, braided, or curly. There is a wave of us who are choosing to "go natural"; to withgo any vigorous forms of hair manipulation. With this new culture, a wave of new haircare entrepreneurs are sprouting up and they are also of the African diaspora. These new CEOs and influencers from the diaspora are creating natural hair care products and tutorials and are putting a dent in the Korean artificial hair market. However, with this new wave of self-acceptance and upward mobility in the African diaspora, there persists the idea that straighter hair is the better hair or, the "good hair".

2

THE PURPOSE OF HAIR

———

It's extremely important to approach this topic fully equipped to prevent oneself against the comfort and trappings of the status quo and/or ego. When we know of our origins, we can make pragmatic choices of what is actually appropriate and beneficial for our lives. Essentially, asking ourselves, 'Is this really okay?' and 'What are the ramifications of this, not just for me but for everyone else?' We live in a very self-centered society where everything is permissible provided it is legal however, permissibility doesn't mean that it is beneficial for everyone. Just because a person can do something doesn't mean they should do it. So, what is the purpose of hair anyway?

Looking at the science of hair, we are aware that hair is a sensory organ which regulates body temperature and also protects us against the sun and wind. We also know that the hair shaft is in its healthiest state when it is hydrated on a regular basis. However, the science of curly hair is more so complicated. Coily hair is able to insulate within the volume of hair to create warmth in cool weather, and is also able to hold moisture for prolonged periods to act as a sort of air conditioner in warm weather. When the coils are straightened by either chemicals or heat [thereby destroying the aforementioned characteristics], humidity in the air replenishes the straightened strands of hair with moisture causing it to revert back to its curly state. When the hair is processed in any way, the shaft becomes brittle and prone to splitting and breakage due mainly to dehydration.

Hair wasn't placed on our heads as an accessory to lure people into our lives as much as we seem to portray it was.

Lost In Tangles

It isn't our hair that keeps that loved one in our life. It is our personality that relates to others such as our own idiosyncrasies that drive some insane and others directly to our side. It is our culture, values, and even hygiene that keeps friends and family in our lives as opposed to the hair upon our head. We may be attracted to a person's image however, once we conversate with them long enough, they began to unfold, and we began to find out who that person really is and subsequently, make the decision as to whether or not we'd like this person in our life.

So as we wear these popular hairstyles that take hours to achieve and discourages any form of exercise, we need to keep in mind the purpose of hair. We need to remember the purpose of hair as we wear these hairstyles so that we won't lose ourselves within them because although it is true that we are not our hair, in a sense we are. We are the fruit of all the hours spent doing our hair and equally, of all those hours not spent exercising or swimming with our family. We may become unhealthy from the lack of exercise and harsh chemicals we may place on our scalps. We may even become resentful or critical of other folks who do not opt to spend as much effort on their hair as we do. With that, the same can be said for people who wear their hair naturally; some natural hair proponents, unfortunately, often criticize non-natural hair women for supposedly "trying to look white".

Furthermore, hairstyles can also leave impressions on people whether good or bad, irregardless of our intent.

However, a constant reminder of hair's true purpose keeps us cognizant of what we could possibly be portraying to the world and what we are genuinely trying to portray. Just because one doesn't find the correlation between self-image and human reaction personally attributing doesn't negate the fact that we are humans reacting to the perceived environment around us. Everything we do affects someone else as well as ourselves but, if we remain true to ourselves and live consciously in every area of our lives including in the decisions of our haircare, we will have achieved true success.

There also lies the argument that hair is just that and nothing more. I agree wholly from the standpoint that hair is as naturally given to us as the world and family in which we were born into. If living with family and community presents a life of difficulty and longsuffering, then we are more likely to find other solutions. Some may choose to normalize the situation and deal accordingly however, others may leave and seek to dwell in a more nurturing environment. The same situation presents itself in regard to hair. Whatever your hair is to you, whether it is straight, curly or wavy, you view it in a certain way. To a person with straight hair styling may not be difficult however, it could still cause one to feel a certain way due to personality. Perhaps, it is difficult for a person with straight hair to feel a sense of uniqueness or specialness and in order to achieve such fulfillment they may seek to curl or cut their hair into a unique style that suits them. Such decisions are justified in that we each give purpose to our own hair. It is to only the beholder of hair to attach purpose.

3

SELF-WORTH WRAPPED IN SELF-IMAGE

There are many in this current society who are in debt by thousands of dollars, in credit cards alone. We are trying to create an image for ourselves of either the perfect family, bachelor or bachelorette and in the pursuit of said there are materials needed to furnish that image. We are conditioned into believing that we need to purchase the latest cars, homes, clothes, make-up, gadgets and even hair, in order to be classified as successful and worthy of attention, not to mention attractability. Images are constantly placed in front of our faces telling us we're not good enough unless we have what they are selling and unless we fit their image. It's quite a dangerous psychology to have your self-worth wrapped up in your self-image.

It is in man's nature to desire new and exciting things and to want to also feel desired and honored in some way however, it is a tragedy when a person is honored not due to character, but due to the self-image he/she has acquired. Straight hair connotes that a person is sophisticated, cultured, amenable, or as some would characterize as "safe" whereas, kinky-curly hair connotes that a person is political, aggressive, and defiant, or "dangerous". To be able to undermine such stereotypes is no easy task and so, requires many to take a stand, however dealing with the consequences of these labels causes one to take pause to question their own self worth. Is my image, which I so love and sometimes causes controversy destroying my self-worth? If something about my physical characteristics is offensive or off-putting to which I may lose friends, family, work, or opportunities, shall I not just change the way I look? In that instance, one is degrading him/ herself. I'll just straighten my hair for the job interview or audition. The exact same can be said for this thought process. The person is still undermining his/her own feelings to cater to the desires of others.

Inquiring within oneself instead of to others should be the very first step in trying to achieve the best outcome. I will not speak of decisions involving special circumstances such as trying to provide for children. A mother will do whatever she has to do to provide for her kids, quite rightly however, it is always well to seek the healthiest outcome for yourself, first. You alone have your best interests at heart, savor that.

It is best to work on your inner self as much as you are working on your outer self, for what good is a big, shiny, red apple if it is spoiled within? The materials we accumulate will fade and become outdated. Straightened and chemicalized hair will eventually weaken and break overtime, and employers who stereotype people will continue until people take a stand for their own dignity. Demand for people to desire to work with you, befriend you or love you on account of who you truly are, as opposed to what you think they would desire of you. Self-worth requires one to be true to him/herself and in doing so, one creates a healthy self-image. Self-worth should in no way be wrapped in self-image, quite contrary, self-image should be wrapped in self-worth. Essentially, the way you see yourself should be wrapped in the good that you are sharing with the world. For instance, it is well for a person to think highly of him/herself if they are volunteering their time, money, or resources to help people, animals, or the environment in any way. Furthermore, when someone is spending their time and resources on others, they are less likely to fall prey to the trappings of materialism and self-comparison because there is less emphasis placed on such. The way a person feels about themselves should absolutely never be wrapped in materialism, aesthetics, or the opinions of others.

4

IMPRESSIONABLE YOUTH

Youth have always been impressionable, however marketing has never been so aggressive, persistent, and blatant. Images are everywhere to never be escaped. They are in our homes, roadways, schools, public restrooms and religious institutions. They greet us when we arise while checking our phones and before we go to sleep, as it is often the last thing we do before turning in. As difficult it is for an adult to mentally censor the images marketing feeds to the world, how much more difficult is it for a struggling adolescent?

The time of adolescence is dedicated to figuring out who you are and what you want to do in this world. It is a time filled of questioning, testing, and challenging the status quo of the world fueled by sudden physical changes within the body. Hormones are raging and emotions are at an all-time high. In this moment, youth can be exceptionally defiant, yet painfully impressionable. So, with these marketing images tag-teaming their minds, in a time when their brains aren't yet fully developed, it can create for a great passive and gullible generation.

The frequency of marketing ads isn't the only culprit, the quality of content also wreaks havoc on young minds. Whenever a teenage girl constantly observes images of models whose bodies are drastically thinner than the normal Body Mass Index and at the same time are being offered praise for their work, it sends ambiguous and confusing messages. Music videos and such often stereotype women and whether or not the intent is obsolete, it encourages young girls to dress in such immodest ways, to prefer slimmer bodies and to praise straight, blonde hair. Men are also falling prey, in the thinking that if they can't provide for all the expenses of the household, even in such an inflated society, then he is not worthy. This is very detrimental to the population as a whole as you can see. Even though there may be diligent parents who recognize this and talk to their children about such images, there still lies the overwhelming amount of advertising that will inevitably haunt our children. Learning to say no is one way to combat, however placing a cap or limits on advertising can also help.

There was a time when television turned off at a certain hour in the evenings. I'm quite sure the rate of insomnia and debt was lesser than it is today. In this day, one can shop online all night and succumb to any amount of images, as well as any content of images as often as they please. Adults and children, alike, are addicted to any and all gadgets. Most homes have a television in every bedroom and an alarming amount of families eat meals apart from each other. This can all culminate into a detached generation.

If the youth of today is made aware of such facets of today's culture and given the tools to combat them, I believe they will be better equipped to cultivate a superior generation. It would better suit this society to implement programs to reach out to the youth to offer them tools to help them process and deal with today's image/technology-driven society. It's a new world out there so, it would be wise of us to properly educate our kids.

Part II

PART TWO

5

MY HAIR JOURNEY

I have always been attracted to fashion. I didn't grow up with much, but I made the best of what I had. If my wardrobe wasn't exciting, my hair was going to be exciting. I took a liking to the hairstyles of Whitney Houston, Mary J. Blige as well as the simplistic hairstyles of Caucasian women I saw on television as a child. I just wanted to feel as beautiful as they looked. I can remember standing in the mirror at the tender age of seven curling my hair with a curling iron. I loved the beautiful curls it produced and how close [in my opinion] it came to resemble what I was intending to achieve.

By the age of eleven, I was applying relaxers and flat ironing women's hair for the price of twenty-five to thirty bucks. Just a few friends of friends I had met in the neighborhood. I had learn it all from my mother who would also teach me to install braid extensions. My work wasn't perfect, and I made it known to my clients but they seemed encouraged by my work on other women's hair as well as my own. My taste in hairstyles changed as my family moved into a more diverse city such as San Diego, as opposed to my predominantly black hometown of Hampton and Newport News, Virginia.

I was exposed to so many different, beautiful cultures and races that expressed themselves in their own unique ways. I fell in love with all of them. I respected all of them. They encouraged me to reflect on my own culture and my appreciation and love for it. However, there was one thing I wished my culture could embrace of its own heritage and that was our hair. I had attended numerous beach parties and pool parties with my multicultural group of friends and loved their carefree sense of hair life. My own hair life seemed as though it was crumbling as the two hydrogen, one oxygen molecule slowly hydrated my beautiful straightened tresses in which accordingly, my once silky straight hair turned into a frightening array of a somewhat straight, wavy and curly bouquet. I wanted a change but I didn't know the right solution.

In the meantime, I began to wear protective styles such as braids more often to reduce the stress of my hair life and to promote that carefree sense I found in my Latino, Asian, Indian, Ethiopian, Chaldean and Caucasian friends. I particularly loved how my Dominican Republican and Ethiopian friends could confidently wear their hair straightened and with just as much confidence wear their hair in its naturally curly state. I craved that freedom, self-love.

Lost In Tangles

After wearing braid extensions continuously for about two years, I removed them to find my hair resembled the hair of my Ethiopian friend, super coily. My hair had grown to the middle of my back however, my newly defined, lucious coils bounced and sat on my shoulders. I was dumbfounded. This is what my natural hair looked like? Had I known, I would have never applied relaxers or flat-ironed my hair, or so I thought. I was so in love with my new length, I wanted to show it to the world, so I flat ironed it…every week. I also utilized the curling iron throughout the week just before wrapping it at night. I wrecked my hair again and had to live through years of damage control.

As a newlywed, I was so excited to show my Caucasian husband all the ends and outs of my culture, especially my hair. I wanted him to love me for me, so I included him in all the processes of my hair. He was fascinated with my tresses in that they could go through so much stress and still decide to stand upon my head. But as life began with him and we began to travel, play at the beach and attend movie nights at the community pool, my craving for that sense of hair freedom hit full force. I wanted my hair to be simple and healthy.

I stopped relaxing my hair and decided to only flat-iron my hair once every two weeks, not to apply any heat in between, regardless. It worked. My hair was once again healthy and stopped breaking, essentially allowing its naturally-fast growth. I continued this for years. I would strategically schedule swimming or any events having to do with water around my haircare regiment. So, if I was washing and flat-ironing my hair on Friday, I would allow my hair to get wet no sooner than Thursday night. It worked however, not without resentment of some sort. Resentment of women who could freely swim or walk in the rain without worrying about their hair getting wet. I loved braids however, they are time consuming when you are such a person who chooses to rebraid your hair yourself due to the fear of someone pulling the edges of your hair out. I grew tired of the routine of braiding, straightening, and of worrying if the humidity was going to affect my hair so I once again sought change.

With motherhood, came my

beautiful children with luscious , curly hair. Their hair isn't as tightly coiled, as they resemble the curls of a young Keri Russell however, you weren't going to comb through it unless it was saturated in water and conditioner. I loved the simplicity of their hair routine. Just once a day and preferably in the mornings, I'd condition, comb out their hair and lightly rinse the conditioner. As their hair was also prone to dryness, I learned to limit washing their hair to twice a month or after swimming. I felt the conditioner washed it enough. The conditioner tended to seal in the moisture and define the curls enough, so I began to leave a bit on their hair. This led me to think of simpler hairstyles for myself.

I still remember the day like it was yesterday. I drove our Toyota Sienna to

Fairfax, CA to Braids by Sabrina hair salon. I was completely done with all the fussing over my hair. Although my hair was near mid-back again, I wanted absolute freedom. I wanted dreads. "There's no going back. Are you absolutely sure you want to do this?", Sabrina asked me with wide eyes. I was absolutely sure and excited for my new, carefree hair life.

I loved my dreads. I felt completely beautiful. I felt relieved of all the hard work I used to pour into my hair. Most of all, I felt natural; the way I felt God intended for me to live. Everyone has a calling on their life and I truly felt this was the way I was to live. I was so happy and joyful about my life.

Seven years later life hit and thus I craved a change, so I combed my dreads out. It took weeks but with my two tiny lice combs (I never had lice but I knew the small comb would work) and many 32 ounce TRESemmé conditioner bottles, I achieved success. My hair only touched my shoulders due to cutting my waist-length dreads into a bob consistently for two years, but I was excited to discover my original curls again. I fell in love with my curls. I no longer wanted to straighten them. I only wanted to condition my hair and apply a cream to hold the definition. I eventually mastered the wearing of what I like to call "wash and go's" and whenever I grew tired I'd wear braid extensions until I also tired of them.

Today, I still favor my wash and go's. I truly miss my dreads and weekly contemplate getting them again, but I absolutely love to play with my coils. I felt that I was still hiding my real hair whilst wearing dreads because no one could see them. I truly adore my coils and never wish to hide them. On occasion, I will blow dry my hair and apply bantu knots at night to take out the following day for an occasion however, I am finally experiencing my real hair and loving it. Even though I have yet to discover all the right techniques and hair products to perfectly define my curls, I love not worrying about swimming, exercising, traveling, the smell of burnt hair and an unwashed scalp. I'm over it, at least in this season in my life. Perhaps, in two months time I will have changed my mind and I find that quite well. However, for now I absolutely love feeling the water flow through my hair every morning and the overall fresh feeling I get from bathing my whole body as opposed to every part with the exception of my hair. I may get more compliments from the smell of my hair than the look of my hair at this point in my journey, and I am quite fine with that.

There is one thing that stood out to me as far as trying to achieve perfectly defined curls. Whilst on the verge of giving up on natural hair due to having to purchase a ridiculous amount of hair products in order to achieve said perfectly defined curls, my husband pointed out to me that it is also ridiculous to try to achieve such a defined curl pattern if it is not already natural for my hair to do so. I was blown away and convicted in my spirit. I had realized that I was still trying to conform to the status quo, subconsciously. And with that, I'm that much more secure in myself.

6

PROCESSED GOOD OR BAD

Processing my own hair came as natural to me as learning to walk. I mimicked what I saw in my world. I knew not that it was good nor bad. Processed hair was just another way to express and to groom oneself. Some people did lavish things with their hair and others did not. The decision was totally fine as long as it lingered somewhere within the range of status quo. As a child and as innocent and loving we are at such an age, if a little girl wore an afro to school I'd chalk it up to her awakening far too late for her mother to properly fix her hair. Although, I wouldn't have discriminated against her decision to wear an afro, it bothers me that I, as a child, would harbor such thoughts. If we search deep within, we would realize that we all have prejudices in one way or another. Even if a family teaches their own to wear their hair naturally, there always lies the risk of said family discriminating those who choose not to. I am hard pressed to make the assumption that a person who does not wear their hair naturally does not love their natural hair. There are many factors at play in a person's choice to process their hair such as time, money or even employment. Our problem lies not in processed versus natural. It lies in the crevices of our own hearts, and it is up to us to sweep clear all the corners that harbor prejudice, discrimination and all others that seek to destroy. For these are the characteristics that perpetuates the wall we place between one another as women and even as men. It is our daily duty to replace these with respect for all.

I can't say that I genuinely felt beautiful when wearing my hair in a processed hairstyle. A huge part of me felt extremely artificial because this was not the natural state of my hair, not to mention all the work I had to do to achieve and protect this processed hairstyle. I felt fearful for any of my nonblack friends to discover my natural tresses. I feared the inevitable inquisition of my hair. Specifically, the famously dreaded question, 'Is that your hair?'. I ended up feeling inadequate around my nonblack friends due to my disingenuity and that particular feeling of hiding or perhaps, protecting, a piece of myself haunted me. I had learned not to sleep or nap in certain positions, to not lay my head on any sort of cushion and I intentionally, swam with a weave. This was all to conceal the natural state of my hair and thus, was incredibly stressful on a preteen who was trying to find herself in life. I knew that this chapter of my hair journey could not last. Something would have to give.

As I aged, I grew more complacent about my processed hair. Don't get me wrong, I enjoyed accomplishing beautiful hairstyles and the challenge of maintaining them however, I loved simplicity more. It no longer seemed normal to wake up to perfectly set hair. I wanted to wake up to normal "bed head" hair or messy hair just like my non-afro-haired friends after a sleepover at church. At that time, I couldn't imagine what my own "bed head" hair would look like since I couldn't remember the natural texture of my hair however, I did know that it would not look pretty and I also knew that it didn't feel quite right to arise out of a sleeping bag with beautifully set hair. In such instances such as swimming or sleepovers, I'd always feel as though my hair were the elephant in the room.

Underneath my desire to awake to messy hair was simply the desire to be free with my hair. In my quest for simplicity, I would revert to wearing braid extensions to experience the freedom of awaking without the worry of if I've flattened a hair track that I had gelled onto a roller set and microwaved for ten minutes or worrying if I had somehow managed to loosen the hair tracks that were glued onto my head. Unfortunately, when glued tracks loosen they have this horrifying potential to curl up, revealing to the world of its presence. I don't know why my complacency towards my hair meant so much to me but I knew it would lead to something more meaningful.

My "cosmetology" days came in very handy as I was called upon to install hair tracks for people to portray Jesus in church plays. I was grateful really for all the techniques I had learned over the years. I'd come to genuinely respect the work of cosmetology however, I had never considered it a calling of mine. I truly enjoyed making people feel good about themselves, no matter how fleeting that feeling was. I wondered just how exactly others dealt with the ever changing life of processed hair. Did they too wonder if there was a better hair journey out there? I find it disturbing that I had never thought to rediscover my natural tresses. Upon reflection, I had a false belief of my natural hair texture. I believed my hair was naturally curly, wavy and straight within the same strand. I didn't know that my varied texture was due to heavy manipulation and hair processing so with that, the object of my obsession at that time was to discover the most convenient, yet beautiful weaved hairstyles so that we too could sleep without hair scarves and swim disencumbered. However, most of all I sought to feel free.

I realized that I was probably projecting my own feelings. I was feeling inadequate because I couldn't express myself through simply wearing my natural hair. I felt stifled. I felt I wasn't being true to myself because I couldn't simply be. If I couldn't be true to myself, how can I possibly be true to my friends and family. As I was brought up with strong morals, such dilemmas chipped at my soul. I hadn't met any other black girls like myself who grew weary of our culture imposed hairstyles. I was a person who cultivated a deep appreciation for life in its purest form and harbored an innate, deep attraction for the simple life. After being born and raised amongst the forests of Virginia, I've since envisioned myself living modestly in a small town surrounded by beautiful scenery.

I've deeply respected nature and have felt that human beings should live as naturally as possible in spite of this modern, technological world. I comprehend it as such, when we are disconnected from nature we began to lose sense of our true selves and role within this world. In our disconnection from nature, we've begun masking ourselves by living in excess of everything from unnatural grooming, to gluttony, as well as materialism. We have televisions in every bedroom and our garages are filled with unused belongings. This way of life is slowly stripping us of humaneness, compassion, and brotherly love which are all needed to pass down to future generations. Materialism is molding us into self-centered, supercilious hoarders. In order to transmit humaneness and brotherly love upon others we must first utilize these same principles upon ourselves. For when we truly love and accept ourselves for how nature made us, only then can we express the same to others. It is only then that we are truly living as we were intended to.

7

FALLING IN LOVE WITH MY HAIR

It took some time after my transition to natural hair to feel as though I had finally perfected the styling of it. I had combed through thousands of pictures of my beloved, simple "wash and go's" and consistently wondered why my hair never took on crisp, defined coils. Whilst my hair definitely displayed a cornucopia of coils, I desired the sleek, defined coils I constantly viewed on the internet. I'd come to realize that in order to achieve such a style many of our naturalistas were using gel. Knowing how drying gel can be and how it would only dry out my already thirsty hair, I made myself steer clear of it and instead, cling to leave-in-conditioners and creams. I also wasn't amused by the smell gels often emit. I felt as if I were a walking chemical stick. Since I only occasionally achieved the crisp, defined coils I so loved, I was rarely ecstatic about my hair however, I continued to wear it naturally because of my values. I truly valued the health of my hair and didn't want to sacrifice it for a hairstyle. So, instead of taking pride so much in a perfect hairstyle, I learned to take pride in the health and sweet smell of my hair, that became beautiful hair to me.

Falling in love with my hair was actually accidental. As I had been sporting "wash and go's" for some time, I would occasionally blow dry my hair to install bantu knots. I loved the medium-sized curls that would manifest in my mid-back hair length. By the end of the afternoon, they'd turn into big, beautiful, voluptuous curls that I really adored. I was so happy to be able to wear a baseball cap [or any hat for that matter] whenever I wanted, and I loved the simple mornings where I could just place my hair in an elegant, high bun, quickly slip on clothes and run out the door. However, I realized that I would always get really anxious after a few days and anyone who has ever had dandruff knows how dandruff often sneaks up on you for you to find yourself anxiously scratching your scalp. In my particular case, I would end up viciously scratching my scalp until it bled because I hated the idea of anything "caking up" on my scalp without my permission, so I inadvertently ended up scraping and scratching off all of the dandruff from my scalp. Of course, it's not bad at all in the less humid, winter months.

Nevertheless, the duration of my bantu knots were getting shorter and shorter and not so much because my head was itching. The shortened duration was due to my missing the feel of water run through my hair and over my scalp every day and the sweet aroma that always followed whenever I wore a "wash and go". I learned to become aware of the smell of my scalp and wasn't pleased with the smell of it after wearing a processed hairstyle for a few days due to not being able to wash my scalp daily or every other day. Once, I tried parting my hair and wiping each and every part with a wet cloth. It worked but, impatiently, I jumped in the shower and drenched my head to get it over with. I kiss my kid's daily conditioned hair when hugging them and I always take notice of their sweet, fresh smell. In spite of running around at school recess, their hair and scalp always carry a sweet aroma which made me rethink my hairstyle choices. I went back to the drawing board and had to reevaluate my choices for wearing processed hair for long durations of time- according to my own values. I had to accept the fact that they were not only unhealthy for my curls nor scalp under long durations, but they also made me self-conscious of my hygiene and I had to process that internally somehow. What did I value in this situation? In the past, I would have valued the hairstyle over the health of my hair. I would have compensated for the disconcerting aroma of processed hair by applying perfume or a sweet, alcohol based hairspray that would mask the smell.

I guess you can say I care more about the emotional and intellectual impact my hair has on someone, including myself, as opposed to what my physical impression conveys. If I can articulate this at all I'd say, sincere and intelligent words followed by a warm embrace in which you are also engulfed by a pleasant smell is my highest desire as opposed to sincere and intelligent words followed by a hesitant embrace in which you are engulfed by chemical smells or worst, the dreaded "burnt hair smell". It's the little things that keep me running back to "wash and go's". Of course, everyone has to discover what makes them most happy for themselves because what is good for one person isn't necessarily good for another. What are your values? What matters most to you? It would be perfect for anyone reading this book to realize what they themselves would write underneath each of these chapters.

8

ROLE MODEL TO MY CHILDREN

Almost every parent reflects on the imprint they are embedding in the hearts and minds of their beloved children. We as parents desire for our kids to become better human beings than we are so we try our hardest to teach them how by having meaningful talks and sometimes by instructing them. However, children are more likely to follow our actions as opposed to what we tell them. Of course, there are many other factors at play, but it is quite well known that we as humans have been mimicking other humans, particularly our own parents for generations.

We all know the famous saying, "Do as I say and not as I do". Well this also falls into play with personal grooming. Many little girls stand and watch with much curiosity as their mother styles her hair and applies makeup. They watch in awe and are eager to do the same thing. I've never liked the idea of letting my daughters play in makeup because I wanted them to feel beautiful the way they are so I'd always decline their request to do so. After I would inform them that they're already beautiful and didn't need makeup, they'd tell me that I too was already beautiful and would continue to request to play in it. They had a really good point however, I would continue to decline, and I eventually learned to apply makeup when they weren't around. By the time my last daughter was born I had a new outlook on life. I bought my daughter her own makeup brushes and makeup when she finally asked to play in my makeup. She now takes her clear mascara wherever she goes. I'd come to the conclusion that it is just art for her and she just wants to play. She didn't see makeup as an adult does which is to accentuate the best features, hide flaws or to possibly lure a man, she simply saw it as another way to play. [I] made it about beauty as opposed to her making it solely about play. She no longer plays in her makeup with the exception of her clear mascara every once and a while however, she now wants to mimic the hair practices of her favorite movie characters by straightening her hair.

Ever since I started having children I set boundaries for myself to prevent my children from following in my unhealthy footsteps. I stopped buying unhealthy magazines that did nothing but provide gossip on celebrities and rave on the current diet trends. I stopped watching TV shows that weren't uplifting or wholesome however, the one thing that haunted me the most and left me feeling evermore helpless was the realization that one day my girls were going to have the desire to straighten their beautiful curls. I dreaded that day so much.

When my oldest daughter was in kindergarten I decided to get dreads. I had entertained the idea for some time and finally felt the strength to go through with it, for good or for bad. No one knows if they will look good in dreads, I certainly didn't but, I was ready for the challenge. I desired simplicity. I wanted to be able to get up and go without the hassle of the very involved process of styling my hair. Styling my children's hair had conjured up a desire in me to wear my hair naturally in some way. I longed to wear my curls but at the time all I knew of was my processed hair that was comprised of three textures within one single strand. I didn't know that a cornucopia of coils were waiting to be discovered so I felt that dreads was the best choice for me.

Dread extensions provided me with everything that I desired. I was able to simply wake up, wash my face, brush my teeth, dress and head out the door. There was no concern about the rain, swimming or exercising. My only concern was when I needed to twist my hair at the roots. Being that my hair grew so fast after getting dreads, I had to twist my roots once every week as opposed to once every month in which I was initially instructed. As my hair grew and fast it did, I cut off the dread extensions and was left with my own hair dreaded although I continued to wrap the outside to provide a thicker dread. I truly enjoyed the simplicity and enjoyed it for years however, I was haunted by the texture of my own hair. I had once seen my hair full of beautiful, defined curls after the "taking down" of my braid extensions. After I started seeing more and more black women displaying their naturally curly hair, I wondered if my hair would look the same. I wondered if I could imitate the same, simple hair routine of my children: condition, comb and out the dome (referring to the head). Furthermore, I wondered if my children would more resemble me with my hair in its natural curly state. My kids are biracial, with their father being white and I, of course, black. Because I am black, I am horrifyingly often thought of as the nanny. That can be extremely frustrating to hear at times because I know they have a lot of my features but the fact that they are lighter in skin tone they are not so readily matched to me. So, although I was a great role model to my children in wearing dreads, particularly in a natural hairstyle, I thought I'd be more of a role model if I would actually learn to style my own natural curly hair. That is to say, only if my natural curl pattern had been restored.

My natural curl pattern was indeed restored and I learned to style it. I feel like I am a stronger role model for my kids now that I am displaying my natural curls because they can see that I too have curls and that I am feeling the same pressures to conform to today's standards as they are. Not to say that this is the only way I can relate to them and encourage them to love themselves, but I felt that my kids would follow my physical example more so than me reassuring them with my words or anything else that wasn't tangible. I felt that I wouldn't have to speak a word. A simple glance at my own natural, curly hair would speak volumes of self love and strong values that could redirect their feelings of inadequacy or possible self-hate.

Since I have been wearing my hair in its naturally curly state for a few years now, my kids have had many questions regarding hair. My kids really love my naturally curly hair and many times state that I shouldn't straighten, braid or even install bantu knots, which would create bigger curls. My son, in particular, hates when I change my hairstyle. He only wants it naturally curly, but he also really misses my dreads, which he affectionately called "pipes". My eldest child would always ask when I was going to take my braids out or stop installing bantu knots. She'd ask, "When are you going to wear your hair curly again?" I try to keep my kids grounded but many times they seem to keep me grounded. My kids know that I too may fall prey to society's standards. I share some of my own insecurities with them and talk it through with them whilst pointing out any irrational thinking I may have and anything conflicting with my morals and values essentially, creating a hands-on learning opportunity. I pray that they will remember and utilize these tools when they too become adults. The vision of a perfect role model is never clear and rightly so because every person is different but as long as a parent is conscious of his/her actions and considers the possible effects on his/her child they are on the right track.

9

OTHER PEOPLE'S OPINION

———

Everyone has an opinion on everything. It's human nature. We may not all make our opinions known to the world but we still have them and that's quite fine. That's what makes us human. We process whatever comes into our mind and filter it as we feel necessary. There are also beliefs and opinions that are passed down from generation to generation whether or not they are truly based on fact. It is all too easy to grant more than enough energy to thoughts and beliefs that are not based on fact, but we need to also remember that even scientists will admit that there is a vast amount of questions they still do not know the answer to. There are also plenty of thoughts and opinions that were once thought to be based on fact but have since been found to be just the contrary. One man's opinion is just that unless he begins to use that opinion to discriminate against others such as the discrimination against African American hair.

To discriminate against a person's natural hair is a bit blasphemous in so that one is essentially rejecting and demeaning "nature" in itself, who provided the elements in which we, human beings and the universe, are made up of. Furthermore, the ethnocentricity of such a declaration is truly abhorrent in so that it unapologetically, audaciously, and confidently makes the cold statement that one person's innate physical nature is superior to another. It is a real injustice to mankind to continue to perpetuate such forms of discrimination and with that said, it would be such an investment to promote our natural, untainted bodies.

The current news of discrimination

against natural black hair in schools and the workplace is very disheartening however, it is good that such problems are coming to the forefront because we all have the opportunity to come together and take this head on. I truly believe that this shouldn't be made to be a "black" or a "white" problem. To the contrary, I believe this is a human problem. It would be to the benefit of the world to hold natural beauty rallies around the world promoting natural hair and body shapes of all cultures. We would then, in essence, be focusing our energy towards positivity, such as learning about others and embracing our diversity, as opposed to holding some sort of a war rally which just promotes hate. When someone publicly approaches a bully and demands their lunch money back, no matter how correct the bully believes his opponent to be, his only focus is that he is being publicly rebuked and shamed and that he needs to do everything in his power to save face. Thus, what was supposed to be an intervention and request for retribution fundamentally turns into an all-out war. However, wisdom tells us that peace and love reach further than the vicious cycle of war and strife. Instead of the all too common cycle between our enemies, we'd have this steeply positive inclination of peace and love to not only solve the issue at hand but to also solve future problems that would inevitably arise.

It is true that peace and respect appears to be more attainable with people other than friends and family members. Most people seem to have this innate form of respect that allows them to disassociate and utilize some form of compassion when faced with the unique choices of others. Such as in the event a previously long and wavy-haired, blonde female student suddenly arrives to class with a buzzed haircut to which she dyed the remaining hair green. Classmates will often be more willing to accept her in spite of her doing, for they are holding to the reality that people need to do what suits themselves as opposed to what others desire of them. In the event of someone's decision that dares to go against the grain, we can apply enough humility to suppress the natural ethnocentrism that may arise and in doing so it will essentially remind us to love each other for who we are as opposed to love being dependent on physical appearance.

I remember going to church long ago with my hair in its semi-natural state. I had a strong desire to wear it no matter the frizz or lack of curl definition. I knew I'd run into naysayers so I wanted to get that over with as soon as possible to just focus on myself. I just needed to do it for myself. I wanted healthy hair no matter what. The moment I walked into the crowd of church-goers, a black, female friend of mine approached me and immediately reprimands me for my natural hair. I was understanding and actually, quite expecting of her response. I had prepared myself that day and so was enabled to feel proud of myself and of my culture, in spite of any dissenters. For a while, some family members continuously asked when I was going to straighten my hair again however, after some time they too have accepted me for who I really am as opposed to this shell that I happen to be in. I feel that I've learned, or taught myself really to dwell lovingly in the person I truly am. I've taught myself to be consciously aware of my own thoughts, feelings, and desires as opposed to denying or critiquing my own thoughts to satisfy and perpetuate the desires of the media.

We have a barrage of other people's opinions attacking our character every single day. Whether it's family or friends, TV shows, billboards, movies, Facebook, Twitter, Instagram, or the person in back of us, everyone wants us to absorb their personal worldview and not only is it unfair, it's not even possible. We all come from different walks of life thus, we have differing opinions, personalities, perspectives and desires. We all see and understand that this world is way too complicated for all of us to agree on everything so, we need to place focus on understanding, embracing, and respecting the differences we all hold. We need to respect the fact that someone doesn't agree with our hair choice or the choice of our wardrobe. However, instead of fighting their opinion we need to accept it for what it is and if it is necessary, enlighten them of our own personal decision. Enlighten people of the nature of your specific hair and what your hair means to you. Teach them the beauty that you see in your own hair. I, myself, encourage people who inquire of my hair to touch it to experience what I love about it. People would see the way my eyes light up when talking about how soft, springy, sweet smelling and freeing my natural hair is. Experiencing my expression of such love for my own hair could cause one to reconsider their own negative feelings towards afro hair in general. People naturally have a fear or disgust of the unknown, so it would be very wise for people to spread the knowledge of unknowns such as afro hair, to dispel any negativity or fears. People shunned the computer until they learned to use it. I've learned to love and celebrate my own idiosyncrasies and physical characteristics and it feels ever so wonderful.

10

WHAT'S BEST FOR YOU

———

Ultimately, you have to decide what is best for you. Decide what makes you feel best about yourself and who you are. No one else can decide this for you. As I've stated before, that which is good for one person isn't always good for another. There are also genuine extenuating factors at play to which you need to consider. Time, money and if wearing your hair naturally would even afford you anymore self love than you already have, would all need to be considered to reach your own conclusion.

It is never an all or nothing decision you are taking on, as some find it best to straighten or blow dry their hair for travels, holidays, celebrations or just to give themselves a much needed change of routine. It is truly fine to make such decisions. Remember, you need to do what is healthy for you. If that means wearing braids or wigs while you are in school, then so be it. No one has the right to take that from you. Take hold of your sovereignty and live the life that you want to live. It may be the healthiest to wear your hair naturally however, if you can't be emotionally healthy at the same time then it isn't the best thing to do, at least not at that specific time.

I wore my hair naturally for two years continuously wearing wash and go's. I needed a change, so I installed braid extensions in my hair and kept them up for about six months. Upon removing the braids, I forgot the routine of my wash and go's and so my hair didn't please me as it did before. I stopped feeling beautiful and attractive however, I continued to wear the wash and go's. As my confidence started to dwindle I knew I needed to make a change, at least until my self-confidence increased. I wasn't going to spend hours installing braid extensions again, so I decided to straighten my hair. During the weeks in which my hair was straightened, I did my best to research "wash and go" routines or other natural hairstyles to try. I was anxious to feel the water run through my hair again so as soon as I remembered my old routine I jumped in the shower to revive my curls. The fact that I sought out my straightening comb is not any sort of an issue because I already have myself sorted out. My feelings were valid and I knew how to process them. I straightened my hair because it was the healthiest resort for me and I began to feel beautiful again. I desired to feel beautiful authentically and that meant I needed to feel beautiful in the natural state in which I was born, so I took action on that. That may not be the same for you and that is totally fine. I am quite sure and aware there will be times in which I need to feel beautiful in my own hair texture and also times in which I do not have that need. You have to ask yourself what makes you feel your healthiest, emotionally and physically.

Remind yourself of the person you are and the person you are striving to be. Close your eyes and imagine you are in a country you've never visited before, where nobody knows your name. Essentially, granting you a fresh start. Knowing that people are far more willing to accept and love you for who you are at first impression, what self-image would you choose? What are these things that would speak to who you really are as a person that you haven't felt safe enough to reveal to your current circle of friends but would reveal to a new circle of friends? Lastly, who exactly is the person to which you would like them to fall in love? Whatever you decide, fiercely embody that person in this exact moment, with no apologies. That, is being true to yourself.

About The Author

L. B. Hamilton has always enjoyed helping others and has now realized that with today's technology it is easier to do so. Fresh on the literary scene, L. B. has a fiction book in the works in addition to this book. She is not new to the music scene however, she has an inspirational album on iTunes under the stage name, Ashira and is currently working on a children's album. She was one of 29 contestants who won a three-week trip to Israel to compete in a

About The Author

global Jewish singing contest and documentary entitled, Hallelujah. She is also the creator of the new YouTube page, Story Time With L. B. Hamilton in which she is able to share her love of reading with children. She is a graduate of Maric College and Ventura Community College and has immediate plans to continue her education. L. B. lives in Ventura, California with her family.

To be in support of L. B. Hamilton, please visit lbhamiltonbooks.com

www.ingramcontent.com/pod-product-compliance
Lightning Source LLC
Chambersburg PA
CBHW062112290426
44110CB00023B/2792